The Night
I Came Out
to God

The Night
I Came Out
to God

J. D. WAGGY

RESOURCE *Publications* • Eugene, Oregon

THE NIGHT I CAME OUT TO GOD

Resource Publications
An Imprint of Wipf and Stock Publishers
199 W. 8th Ave., Suite 3
Eugene, OR 97401

www.wipfandstock.com

PAPERBACK ISBN: 978-1-6667-3503-1
HARDCOVER ISBN: 978-1-6667-9164-8
EBOOK ISBN: 978-1-6667-9165-5

JANUARY 7, 2022 10:49 AM

"Relatable" was originally published in the online *Crux Literary Journal* in March 2015 (https://cruxliteraryjournal.wordpress.com/2015/03/04/relatable-by-j-d-waggy).

"Prayers," "Incompatibility," and "Unthreatening" were originally published in *Unbound* in September 2019 (https://justiceunbound.org/the-umc-and-a-poetic-lament/).

For Barry T. Petrucci, who fights for me in the spaces where I cannot go and fights with me in the moments I forget where God calls me;

and for Mel Lowery and Siddig El Fadil, who keep accidentally teaching me what grace looks like and how Church could be. Shukran, my friends.

CONTENTS

Part Two

⋅⋚ LITURGY ⋚⋅

Part Three

⋅⋚ WORKSHOP ⋚⋅

Preface

WHEN I WAS IN ELEMENTARY SCHOOL, my mother took a part-time job as an events janitor in a large United Methodist church on the south side of the city. Since I was young but not small, I often went along with her as extra, free labor. I would have the jobs of sweeping away the rice from the patio after the weddings or finding all the bulletins in the arced rows of chairs from the funeral or vacuuming the long, long aisle so that all the flower petals were caught.

I hated vacuuming the most.

Once I had finished my jobs, however, I was free to occupy myself until my mother finished her work. Sometimes I would go to the church library and read about the women of the Bible who were strong and fierce like I wanted to be, but often I would go into the sanctuary and play with God.

It sounds odd, as an adult, because we adults do not use the language of play all that often when we talk about God, but there is no better descriptor. I would play hide-and-seek in the lengthening shadows tumbling through the towering stained-glass windows; I would set races around the chair blocks I soon memorized better than the halls of my own house; I would create elaborate stories of exploration as I crawled across the chancel in a way that was absolutely forbidden on Sunday morning but was a safe secret with God on Saturday night. It didn't matter that I was a child in those moments of play, that I fidgeted too much during services or didn't like wearing dress clothes or found Sunday school unnerving because I felt like such an outsider. When it was just me and God in the sanctuary, I could be the entire reality of myself and God didn't seem to mind. In fact, God was a pretty good playmate—very good listener, too.

A quarter century later, I am a pastor in The United Methodist Church and I spend a good many Saturday nights and Sunday mornings and Tuesday afternoons in the sanctuary, but it is not often that I play. I no longer fidget much and I've made a certain kind of peace with dress clothes, but the way I encounter God and the way the Church wants me to encounter God are still at odds. I am, you see, bisexual—and genderfluid, both words that don't exist in Scripture or in the *Book of Discipline*, a pair of documents some hold as equal in their directive power. I cannot professionally be the entire reality of myself and the Church is tearing itself apart about people like me. There are a great many broken hearts because our sanctuaries are battlegrounds; we only play *hide* from each other when it is dangerous to want to be sought, and the light from our stained-glass windows casts an awful lot into shadow.

Poetry is play in language; it is leaping into a ball pit of words and creating something that lives in the spaces prose cannot touch. Poetry is how I remind myself of wonder, how I allow myself to grieve, how I bridge the space around the Holy when I can no longer let myself feel free enough to play hide-and-seek in the stained-glass shadows. So when I thought about how to be present for myself, my congregation, and my fellow LGBTQ Christians as we join all the other denominations that have split over identity, the only thing that made sense was poetry.

I intend this to be a resource. It is written by a Methodist with Methodists in mind, but it is also written by a person with people in mind; this is a starting point for conversation, worship, and experience for anyone standing at the intersection of the cross and the rainbow. I write from a position of being a white, female-presenting United Methodist, knowing that there are some voices in which I cannot speak but who, in the grace of the Spirit, need to hear that they are beloved creations of God. For denominations that have already been through this gauntlet, I write. For those who have not even begun to have this conversation, I write. This is for the queer folk who do not think they can be Christian; for the Christian folk who have been told they cannot be queer; and for the allies who seek to be in conversation and relationship with us, learning the experience behind the buzzwords and issue headlines.

The first section, the poetry, is grouped according to the words in the Methodist *Book of Discipline* that have caused so much heartache and controversy: "self-avowed practicing homosexuals are not to be certified as candidates, ordained as ministers, or appointed to serve in The United

Methodist Church."[1] The poems take on what it means to be "self-avowed," "practicing," and "homosexual," adding to the ongoing conversation not complete definitions but lived experiences of relational humanity. They are ways to remember that queer Christians are not paragraphs in a document but real, breathing, hoping, grieving children of a three-in-one and one-in-three God.

The second section includes liturgy—the work of the people—for any church wanting to hold a service of acceptance and welcome or wanting to include more language of deliberate inclusion in worship settings. Whether your denomination has already split or is currently splitting or hasn't thought about splitting at all, worship services are a beautiful and important way to take a statement of welcome and make it a deliberate act. Worship is our offering to God as people of faith and being deliberate about who is named there is one of the strongest demonstrations of inclusion we have. There are also brief suggestions of how to use the poetry here to create liturgy of your own. Liturgy is poetry, so sometimes it is most helpful to use poetry as liturgy.

The third section is a guide for using this as a small group study or a single-day workshop. There are two tracks: one of discussion, and one of creation. The first includes suggestions for how to allow the poems here to create avenues of expressing the ways we live in Christian community with each other—or do not—and how a church can become a welcoming and safe space for LGBTQ people. The second coaches participants in creating their own poetry, their own play in language that expresses their engagement with the Holy.

Appendix A is an extended bibliography for the larger conversation of inclusion and welcome. It is there that you will find books on how we as a faith got to this place of exclusion and grief because I am not interested in explaining that in this volume. I start with the assumption that you, dear reader, are either LGBTQ yourself or are working toward being an ally. If you are neither of these, this book will likely be a bit much for you. You are still welcome to read it, but understand that I will not be explaining why it is okay for me to be bisexual and a preacher or genderfluid and faithful. There are also resources in this appendix for congregations who are looking to deepen their work in partnership with queer Christians, whether in supporting organizations doing the important ministry of protection and education or beginning teaching ministries and small group connections

---

1. *Book of Discipline* 2016, ¶ 304.3.

of your own. For those who wish to find other poetry resources to read more or write your own, there are suggested books of poetry and sexuality, poetry and religion, and the craft of being a poet.

Last but not at all least, I have included a glossary (Appendix B). Language is a living thing, so I understand even as this book goes to print that some of the terms I define may not mean the same thing in two years, five years, ten. But for right now, I want to give those who are new to some of this terminology as much of a shared base as I can so that you are able to confidently join the conversation of identity.

Wherever you are, beloved sibling, welcome. Welcome to my journey, welcome to this sanctuary, welcome to the reality that the Spirit is still inviting you to play with Her, delighting in the entire reality of you in this dance of shadow and light.

Part One

POEMS

Self-Avowed

CLOSETED

What if I didn't wait for the right
moment, didn't plan a party to say
I'm not as straight as I'd told you;
what if I put no rainbow on my
profile, no ribbon of pride tied around
the handle to my walk-in closet
where the shoes do not judge me—
what if, instead, I painted three
purple flowers and published them
in a journal for queer folk's art?
Would that be enough for you
to let me stand here, just as I am,
one hand trembling on the doorknob?

OUTED

"If your sibling sins against you, go and point out their fault
when you are alone together. If they listen to you, then
you've won over your sibling." Matthew the tax collector
wrote a Jesus who loved sinners and children as though
relationship was better than being right—how quaint.
You brandish your Bible like a bullwhip cracking open
my bared skin once you've hauled me to the town square,
carving a garish rainbow into my chest to warn the others.
You came for me without warning, self-appointed secret
police dragging a woman to the feet of the Church to say,
"Let us stone her, this sinner, this brazen Eve fallen from
the garden we protect with our swords of anonymity."
In front of God and everybody you strip my self to nothing
but sexuality, taking even my name and surely Matthew's
Jesus did not start by saying that if a sibling has sinned,
crucify them in the court of public opinion because
Matthew's Jesus loved children and sinners and
taught that talking to someone first wins them far
better than shaming them into fearful obedience.
But I cannot listen to you telling everyone else how I'm
going to Hell without thinking you will be alongside,
fellow sinner, for I have loved beyond your heterogeneity
and you have ignored the Jesus who loved sinners and
children and said the humble will inherit the Kingdom,
the Shepherd who seeks the one sheep and rejoices.
So we shall face God's judgment together and I hope,
my sibling, that you do not refuse mercy with the same
anger that prevented you from coming to me to point out
my supposed fault, that kept you from honoring the fact
that I, too, am a child of the God we both claim to follow.

A LITTLE BIT FREE

But tonight I dance with broken feet
and feel the music's sway—
tonight I challenge all to meet
the fierceness of my way.
Tonight I fling my arms out wide
and exhale to the sky—
tonight I'm on my own damn side
and refuse your caging "why."

POSITIVE ANTHROPOLOGY

Oh, sinner man, who lives as though you're good—
what ways do you insist upon your soul?
For none but God can name you by a "should"
yet all proclaim your lessness as their goal.

Oh, sinning woman, bold within your faults,
whose heart beats strong to say you are not less—
o'er what broad walls of heaven are your vaults?
From what deep strength do you this faith profess?

These humans fair who innocence proclaim
when others would the narrative enforce
that all are broken, lost, unholy bane—
how do they navigate this rocky course?

Perhaps with hearts unbowed they stand to dare
that those who judge as though of God, beware.

SUPPORT

Yes, thank you, I appreciate the support, I'm so glad
you reached out, thank you, thank you, thank you
stranger I've never seen, person who barely knows
my name, faceless entity that supports the idea of me
without knowing that I hate talking to strangers and
thanking people over and over again for supporting
this beautiful concept of someone I have never been.
I do not know how to tell you to keep doing the work
but not with me, not for me as I slink back into shadows
that never tell me who I should be, that never take one
piece of me and extrapolate an entire entity, that don't
take my face but not my smile to make it a billboard
for a cause no one asked me if I support. I cannot say no
to you, to the support that I need to stay alive, stay
employed, stay human in the world that tells me I am
less, tells me I am something to be packaged and sold
on the market of causes so that you can look at me and see
someone else. I cannot say no to your desire to support
your sister, your best friend, your cousin, your student
who didn't have the help you're offering now, who died
a little bit more every day that they were stripped bare by
the people who did not see they were more than, so much
more than sexuality, color, gender, age, each reduction
taking a little more of the soul their detractors insisted they
did not have. I cannot say no to you and I cannot say enough
that these good intentions are crushing the air from me just as
surely as the people who do not ask me my name, do not ask
before they strip me bare in front of you and show the places
where a soul would be, if I had one. I am just as naked when
you take my clothes to sew a pride flag as when they take
my dignity to say I never wanted to be known like this,
thank you, thank you, please do not call me to talk about
the pieces of my soul I never wanted in the public square.

7

AT THE HANDS OF PONTIUS PILATE

The red line down my sternum from your ungainly scalpel
paints an arrow to the organs that obsess you, possess you,
enflesh me in this cage you think you understand while
breaking open my ribs to crush the heart you never understood
that loves the people you tell me are wrong for me, are wrong
in general. Pilate tried to barter Jesus from the crowds but I
am begging you for myself because cutting me open while I am
still alive kills us both, my death on your soul at the judgment
seat where no one is left unseen by the Jesus who hung naked
as you are trying to make me, stripped bare while soldiers
gambled for the beautiful robe all in one piece unlike Jesus
and me and the ones you insist on shattering. You will not find
the sickness you are searching for that kills any hope of salvation;
there is no evil here, there is no murderer but you, I am not dead
yet. I refuse the descent into the Hell that has risen to meet
me at your hands while you tell me that this is for my own
good, this intervention, this attempt to put me on straight
paths that lead to the god you invented to bless your autopsy
on this heart that loves too much for your unholy scriptures.
The naked Jesus asked forgiveness even for the ones gambling
under the slowly dripping blood that washes away sin but I
do not know how to pray that God should forgive you when you
cannot even say my name as you cut me open, a single red line
you wash from your hands as though my being is what sullies them.

ADDRESS

Someone asked my pronouns and it was easy
for them, this curiosity that didn't used to exist,
this recognition not to judge a book by its cover.

Someone asked my pronouns and it was hard
to know what to say as I wondered for the first
three seconds if I could say something new.

Someone asked my pronouns and it was strange
to think that maybe I could be him, or they, or zhe
if I really wanted it, if I was ready to be myself.

Someone asked my pronouns and it was inevitable
that I would answer she/her as I always have because
I will only be ready to be myself when I have any idea

who that might be, this beloved creation with pronouns
and the brimming desire for someone to ask as though
they honestly want to hear her/xir/my true answer.

FIERY

The meme suggests I live like leaders would have burned me
four hundred years ago, wild and ungovernable, and I don't
know how to say that I'm not even trying that hard but these
leaders of right now still want to burn me, wild and ungovernable
creature that I am simply by existing as someone, by refusing
to stop existing as my multiplicity of selves who are all suspect
for our shared commitment to living. Wildness was assigned to me
by the religions that preached faithful obedience when they meant
voiceless subservience; ungovernability was branded into me
by the power structures that encouraged our patriotic support
when they meant unquestioning assimilation; and no one burns
in the streets at the stake anymore but the meme doesn't cover
the fact that it is four hundred years later and the fires are not
about killing the defiant but consuming the idea that the leaders
are the ones who get to strike the match on those of us who live.

THE NIGHT I CAME OUT TO GOD

The night I came out to God,
the air was so thick it held the stars in place,
pressing warm on my chest like a lover.
Passing headlights dashed across shadowed tree leaves
and Tennessee cicadas rasped good night to the crickets—
all God's creatures got a place in the choir.

The night I came out to God,
I wanted to be polite and proper, my Southern manners
making me wonder if I should wear my church clothes
like God and the preacher expected me to be tidier than this.
I went to God's house to deliver the news properly, in person.
If God ate, I'd've brought pie.

The night I came out to God,
the church was locked.

I sat on the wall that keeps the city out,
looking at the stars in the thick air and trying to breathe
through the tightness, glad I hadn't worn my church clothes
or brought pie. I wondered if cicadas and crickets have identity crises,
singing softly to themselves that the Bible they can't read says
Jesus loves them.

The night I came out to God,
I said to hell with politeness—what I had to say
ain't much polite anyway. I pushed my palms against
the rough stone of the wall and peered at the still leaves
of the tree bending low like a confessor and I told
the God of the stone and the tree and the stars

I don't think I fit who you meant me to be.

The night I came out to God,
I said, "I love that you made man,
strong and bright and complex."
I said, "I love that you made woman,
fierce and resilient and quick."
I said, "I love, and I love and I love and I love
both, and I was wondering if I still
got a place in your choir."

The night I came out to God,
an ant crawled over the sun-warmed wall
and the crickets and the cicadas sang to the summer-still leaves
and the stars winked at the closed-up church
and God said, "Thank you for coming to my house to tell me
in person, just as you are. Some sing low, and some sing higher,
and some love and love and love and child,
all my creatures got a place in my choir."

ON THE EVE OF NATIONAL COMING OUT DAY

Tomorrow, ribbons of color will dance in the rain,
God's promise never to destroy by water flowing
in rivers of laughter and bright stripes down photos,
memories, declarations. Our electronic social clubs
will proclaim You Are Welcome Here, profiles turned overnight
into Roy G. Biv's limitless canvas, #ComingOut, #BeLoved,
only the colors visible as the algorithms quietly hide dissent.

Tomorrow, it will seem like the world takes all the closet doors
and breaks off the hinges, tosses them into a bonfire and dances
in celebration that love is love is love is love, the flames not
destruction but desire licking the tips of the stars and some
will celebrate anniversaries, some will gather new courage to ask
will you join the dance with me, some will stand for the first time to
name themselves in the festivities across the internet into the streets.

Tomorrow, I will read the posts and tweets and snaps and likes and I
will celebrate with those who put aside the fear for today, those who
choose to see beyond the fact that they can be fired, they can be cast out,
they can be dehumanized, they can be told that God may not destroy by
water but they have called down Jehovah's righteous fire, the flames not
desire but destruction licking the tips of the stars—and for another year
tomorrow I will stay silent because the day after, it is safe behind this door.

OUT

It was a cabaret on Coming Out Day and the mic was open
and I had a poem about love and identity and a bit of hope
but it was livestreamed, this cabaret. I could not come out
that far to do this *cha-cha* on Facebook with my skirt ruffling
across Twitter to the world on YouTube beyond this cabaret.
I could only slide one stockinged leg out of this closet, hand
gripping the door so I could slam it shut before anyone tried
to drag me out with certain directions on who I am supposed
to be when in these *cha-cha* skirts of identity's colors, how I
should name myself when it's Coming Out Day at a cabaret
that celebrates openness like a promise, a declaration of
independence that sparks a war I do not have enough blood
to fight. So the open mic welcomed other poets and the live
stream watched lazily with the world to whom I could not show
myself as I slowly pulled my stockinged leg back to these
safer shadows, closing the door just enough to see a bit of light.

JUDICIAL COUNCIL

It is not that you call me illegal, I with my peach-white skin
who has never crossed an imaginary border seeking
another way home as the king kills my kind in search
of the threat I will pose one day. It is that I am named
incompatible, unable to be called by God because man
created the Church when the Spirit danced on people's
language-loosened tongues and we told her to call back
when she understood our restrictions on who is worthy.
To be wholly welcome, I must be half of myself, quartered
and drawn by the horses galloping away from this reality
that you want me to look but never touch, love but never
speak, feel but never hold, be but never become, one flesh
remaining cleaved only to itself. It is the law, they say,
and Paul's insistence that he does not live under the law
trickles through the back of my mind where incompatibility
does not find a foothold amidst the many ways you want me
to hold this Spirit-burned tongue lest I point out the fact
that I am not called illegal with my peach-white skin
but my blood-red heart is impolitely breaking your rules.

DISCOVERY

I've been coming out my whole life,
piece by piece—a mail-order bisexual
earned one sent-away box top at a time.
For the first top, I kissed a woman; my lips
were pleased, but maybe only my lips were gay.
It couldn't be any more of me in 90s Indiana where
you were straight or going to Hell with the Catholics.
Bi was not real, yet (if it's real now, if we can say yes
to both monogamy and duality, if box tops earn
pink and blue decoder rings like they're equal). Bi was
curious, experimenting, straight with an edge like
the velvet Elvis no one bought but everyone had
in their garage sales. In college a girl slept next to me
in a twin bed, shunning her boyfriend; I was always
the big spoon, arm draped over her shoulder.
My left arm and lips were gay but gay was not straight
and bi was not real. I needed more box tops.
In graduate school I realized my heart was in
someone else's hands; she had twisted it and
he had gently set it down, so perhaps my ventricle
is straight but the atria are gay and I keep
finding new ways to come out, new pieces of me
that bend this either/or and I wonder if I just
don't have enough box tops to send away yet,
faulty decoder rings unhelpful in this mysterious code.

Practicing

VULNERABLE

You ask me to be vulnerable—it comes
from "wound" in Latin, you know, *vulnus,*
vulneris. I tell you that vulnerability is
a loaded gun with named bullets; how can
you ask me to put that in your hand and trust
that you will aim for the apple, not my heart,
that you will not even pull the trigger?
Love, you say, but love is a pop song falling
off the back of a pickup truck; love is the
currency you trade when you haven't eaten
in four days; love is what people tell me
has made it possible to keep a marriage,
survive a tragedy, achieve success, and I don't
know why that kind of love doesn't live with me.
My love sometimes can't get me out of bed
and it cannot make me strong enough to stand
still while handing you a loaded gun and trusting
that you have the kind of love that keeps you
from shooting me, my wounds silently dripping
on the floor while I wait, trembling, vulnerable.

DATE

She told me I was cute, even funny, and I told her
I was dangerous. Not in a sexy way, I said, but as
a liability, a quicksand trap, a minefield where she
would only get hurt. *But it's not like that anymore,*
she tried to reassure me, because she sees the pride
flags and the Supreme Court rulings and the rainbow
capitalism that sells us on billboards one month out
of twelve, and I told her I live in the exception to the
ruling, the religious freedom to ensnare, it's not you
it's me except it isn't really me either because I thought
she was cute, even funny. I am a woman and she is
a woman and the god made of printed words and
paragraph citations thinks women are abominations,
thinks women loving women are abominations (forgive
the indistinction because I am still unsure whether this
god is merely tolerating the fact that women dare to
exist in this world of the father god who art in heaven).
So you see I think you are cute, even funny, but I cannot
let them crucify you on the cross beside me because I
cannot promise this day you will be with me in paradise
when I am still trying to dodge the sifting ash of Hell
where an angry god says neither of us is cute, or funny,
or worth being loved exactly as we are with our hands
slightly brushing as we walk too close before I have to say
I'm sorry, it's not you, it's the Church that pays me to hide
that I think you're cute, even funny, and far too beloved
for me not to try to save you from the danger of the idol
that has taken up residence in an empty tomb and proclaimed
all have fallen short of the glory of heterosexual expectations.

PASTORAL CARE

I sat with her shy soul a moment as it asked
if it was okay to break, to be broken, to bleed on the
healed scars of God's hands, to be too human.
"Yes," I said to all of who she was in that moment,
to the grief that rolled into her tears, salt of this earth;
"yes," I gave permission. The shy soul shuddered at being
seen, welcomed, allowed and she thanked me for saying
that God does not hate us for being human, that humans
do not have to make ourselves into unfeeling gods.
"Yes," she said when I asked if she wanted to pray
and we asked the scarred God to make space for
the shy soul wanting to be put back together, gently,
rivulets of grief-salted tears watering the hope
of a God who loves all of who we are in this moment.

INCLUSIVE

All are welcome, welcome in this place—
but only if you don't force us to take it
outside, to proclaim it to the community
beyond our sanctuary, to declare it on a sign,
a banner, with a flag, an emblem crying
"we are That Church," The Gay Church
as you though you can catch sexuality from
symbols. "Get the shotgun, Martha, the
queers are comin' to take us over" runs
underneath your insistence that we shouldn't
push too far, that we welcome everyone but
quietly, that we put our light under a bushel
in this city on a cul-de-sac. You fear that
declaring that kind of welcome excludes
and you're right because hate cannot sit
in a pew next to love and say everything is
fine here. Prejudice cannot dehumanize a child
of God and say *we are both faithful together.*
We cannot tell each other that all are welcome
but only if we can keep the welcome quiet
lest we become known for being That Church
that says blessed are the specific types of people
for theirs is the Kingdom of Heaven; welcome.

TOLERANT

"But I welcomed you—I never told you you were evil,
I visited you when you were sick, I accepted you, how
dare you say I did not do enough." You loved me when
it was convenient, when you knew my name, overlooked
how much of me you did not want to understand, protested
that I should be grateful for the fact that you did not cast me
out of your life because you could have, I know, it is only
fair that people like me recognize that your tolerance is a gift.
So you say when you vote for someone who dehumanizes me
or do not speak up as someone dismisses me; you insist that
it is not really about me. You loved me, after all, and why
can't I see that you have done everything right by me except
anything that asks you to protect me when I cannot speak
in the places where others see tolerance as the ceiling rather
than the floor that I am asking you to walk on instead of my
back that breaks under your insistence that you love me and
people like me who are not like you, you who loved when it was
convenient rather than when I asked you to be more than tolerant.

LATE NIGHT

You fell asleep, head warm on my chest
and it didn't matter that my shoulder ached
or the film ran straight through the credits
or the DVD menu repeated its loop twice
or that I needed to head home on this work night
because you were asleep, and I wanted nothing
more than to see us breathing together, chests
rising in matched slow rhythm, your hair
draped over your cheek, your head warm
against the steady beat of my full heart.

WARNING

This is why they call it a trigger:
someone, something, pulls just enough—
a sentence, an image, a sound, a touch,
*click***boom** the bullet of memory fires,
a hollow-point exploding in your mind
shredding your lungs, stomach, heart.

There is so much blood when you are shot.

It pools amid the fragments of who you
used to be before the bullet, the trigger,
the need to stand still while people ask
are you okay—no. I am dying, bleeding out
where you cannot see, someone pulled the trigger,
but I always say *I'm fine,* it's fine, I have

survived being shot a thousand times before.

DOMESTIC

The rag in the glass spurts water, the physics of displacement,
the soapy shoot spraying across my shirtfront. I hear in the back
of my mind your tongue clicking in resigned recognition, voice
always mild in its condemnation: "You'll never get a husband
with a shirtfront like that, granddaughter. Men like a tidy woman."
The disappointment burned with every new sink full of dishes,
my hands as red as my face at hearing how unlovable I would be.

My wife slides her arms around my ribs, just above the soap,
resting her chin on my shoulder and squeezing me gently. "You
have been playing with the wineglasses again," she laughs, and
I tilt my head back to rest on hers, leaning into her embrace,
my soaped finger drawing a lazily clear hum from the glass in
my hand, my back warmed by the arms just above the shirtfront
that she has never seemed to think was too untidy to be loved.

BEDROOM

"I really don't know why people care so much about
what you do in the bedroom," says the ally, and I
know he is trying to be helpful, trying to be supportive.
I do not know how to tell him he is making this worse,
buying into the narrative that sexual identity is only
sexual and never identity. I think of my first love
whose hair never tangled in my fingers, long and shining
from her meticulous care; I think of how she tasted
of Dr. Pepper Chapstick when we kissed and told ourselves
we were only experimenting, it was practice for the boys,
of course we were straight, of course we had to be.
I really don't know why people care so much about
whether I knew the feeling of her heat, whether I
knew her biblically when the Bible is so vague on women,
anyway. I do know that my grief over our lies to each
person who asked us (including ourselves) is not from
whether I had sex with her but how much I wish
I could have kissed her before a final exam for luck,
I could have taken her out for Valentine's Day dinner,
I could have held her hand when we went to a movie,
I could have asked her to dance with me at prom,
I could have loved her outside on the front porch
and cared very little about what we did in the bedroom.

FIRST

Her name was Samantha, that summer.
We sat on my bed cross-legged,
fun-house mirrors of each other—
she gangling thin, I improbably round,
our bodies as uncertain as we were
about who we were becoming at this
cavern's edge of puberty. We mapped each
other's bones with curious fingers, skin on
skin just hot enough to clash with the
air conditioning raising gooseflesh against the
soft, downy hair we hadn't yet learned not to have.
I knew that day that I wanted to use my lips,
not fingers, to trace the lines of who she was
becoming; that I wanted to say she was beautiful.
I knew that day that she only wanted to know
if I was strange like her, female like her, changing
like her, uncertain like her about who she was
becoming. We sat naked on my bed, one skinny,
one well aware that wanting was not allowed—
so I kept my lips and tongue and wonder to myself,
my fingers tracing her bones under chilled skin.

OUT IN PUBLIC

The drink had a scandalous name,
chauvinism cloaked as cleverness,
but I ordered it anyway—I can only
fight the patriarchy so much, I guess.
I made a joke about it and you asked how
could I know to make a joke like that; I
didn't answer but winked and the conversation
rolled on in stormclouds blowing across our lips.
Maybe you weren't really asking, or maybe I
wasn't really joking, or maybe I just can't parse
you well enough anymore to know if you still
read me like the dog-eared favorite I used to be
before I translated myself into a language foreign
to you. Besides, I couldn't *really* tell you how
I knew about the girls in the drink's name,
how I have kissed the alcohol from their lips
hidden under lies that it was for the boys,
it was for curiosity, it was just an experiment,
it was only us getting it out of our system
before we really understood who God wanted
us to be with our husbands and 2.5 children.
I couldn't *really* tell you that it was always
for the taste of a beautiful woman, full-bodied
as a deep merlot; that it was for the frothy foam
of a girl, sweet as a strawberry daquiri. I couldn't
really tell you about the good, old-fashioned
Biblical joy in the series of Eves on whom dawn's
light never shone. Would you have held my
delight for the way they tasted, rich and real?
Would you have held my sorrow that I don't
even remember their names, these women
from whom I learned to make scandalous jokes
but never learned that I could desire them in
daylight, our minds clear and our love tasting
like fresh water over our parched tongues
wanting only to speak love like God wanted?

Homosexual

IN FUTURE

"Nah—today I'm aromantic," says the girl
casually, identity fluid as the ocean, changeable
as a t-shirt, and I gape. I have learned I am
an elder in the queer community—not from
wisdom but because I am still living beyond
the average of LGBTQ people. It is 28.
My girl-self watches this girl-self who switches
casually to something new, exploring those
t-shirt flags of striped colors, and I remember
how dark it is in the back of the closed-door
closet, scrunched in the corner with the t-shirts
whose colors I didn't yet know in this language
we didn't yet have, locked in the binary of straight
and terribly wrong. I realize I hate her, this girl
with her casual exploration as though we elders
are not still fighting to be called young, as though
I am not still fighting to be called fully human
while she trades labels like lip gloss flavors.
I realize I love her, this girl with her casual
exploration because this is who we are fighting for,
this girl who is almost halfway to being an elder
herself, this living monument to the demolition
of the closet where she will not stay scrunched
but will invent an entire new language of being.
We who are still fighting marvel at all we wanted
being voiced in a steam-warmed kitchen by a girl
who is the wildest dream of us still-living ancestors,
who says "today I am" as though tomorrow is
actually possible, new, unknown, beautiful.

TRANSIENT

I read about the scars on other people's chests,
scorched white double U's underlining the text
of who they know they are, damn the genetics,
and I wonder what it would feel like—trailing fingers
down the ridges like exterior ribs where mountains
used to rise above the too-round plain of my belly.
I read about the growth that mimics but never
becomes, this third leg brushing against the joy
of being in a body that makes sense. I read about
the idea of being settled, known, *right* and I think
it would be nice if I could be surgically reknit into
something that felt like home, a body that felt like
mine, top and bottom something that I present
as though someone else would love it, as though I
could. But they do not make the surgeries for
the scars I want that excise the things I don't,
the growth changing me into something I can
live in, this bone-house of incorrect flesh, this
muscle-suit that allows me to read about scars
and growths and other people who find themselves
in ways that make me wonder what it would feel
like if I knew who I wanted to be, scarred and beautiful.

INDIGO

Roy G. Biv, my father taught me, the strange name
of the non-existent man who plans the prismed light
that splits the sky; this is God's covenantal promise not
to destroy the world that is very good. To me, Roy
made sense—it was something I could see, was right in
a world where wrong was so readily identified, was rules
like chartreuse never next to green because it couldn't
be. Roy was right there—but no one could explain
indigo, the not-blue violet or unviolet blue that threw
a vowel in for easy reading of a non-existent name. I
did not understand indigo but it was right—it was in
Roy's name (which is different than being in Jesus' name
but possibly just as binding). No one could show me
indigo that was different than purple or blue and I
stopped asking, wondering if I didn't have the right
eyes, wrong rods and cones for the job of seeing—
after all, there were so many other things people were
happy to tell me were not the way God intended, faults
picked out in Jesus' name but probably not Roy's.
I no longer looked for indigo, content with binary
blue and purple bleeding into the arc of the rainbow
over which bluebirds flew, somewhere. Roy would be
fine; the human tongue can elide vowels. Until—until
I grew up and grew out and grew beyond the boundaries
of Roy and the binary where possibilities lived in shades
and the Spirit danced in indigo, her hope flying loose
as she celebrated even chartreuse next to green. "Roy
is a beginning," she sang to me with the joy of One who
knows the end and loves the story in the middle because
it is very good. When I was a child, I spoke as a child, learning
that Roy was a prism of light in every 25-cent box of Crayola's
classic lineup—but when I am a man, a woman, a wealth
of possibility, I learned that there are Crayola boxes of 152
shades; I learned that "wrong" is so much more complex
than chartreuse next to green; I learned that my eyes are

not faulty because God's creation is very good and God does not wait for my permission to set a bow in the clouds over infinite diversity in infinite combinations because God is not limited to Crayola boxes or mnemonics and the Spirit dances in indigo even though I still don't see it. It could even be Jesus' favorite color, there in the belly of the rainbow over which bluebirds fly and "right" is a word used sparingly and indigo might be the color of grace.

REVOLUTION

"Be revolutionary," they tell me; "burn down the house
that does not welcome you." Anything less is complicit
in the status quo, acceptance of being less than human,
as different as They have made me—this society from which
I am apparently always meant to stand apart, to threaten.
The enthusiasm burns me, not the house, because I am
revolutionary every time I get up in the morning and live;
I am radical simply by existing in all the spaces I am told
to burn to the ground, and I am so damn tired of saying
it is enough to stand here, breathing in bisexual genderfluidity,
burning nothing at all save for everyone else's expectations.

BYSTANDER

It was almost as though you loved her—
the way your heart soared when she smiled,
leaning into the life that sparked and shone
in a guiding beacon to her wandering soul.
(*Come home, come home*, you cheered. *Be well.*)

It was almost as though you loved her—
the way your heart broke when she smiled
but not with her eyes, when her laugh
was as brittle as her embrace, the cuts fresh.
(*Come home, come home*, you begged. *Be well.*)

It was almost as though you loved her—
the way your heart fell when she smiled
in bitter mockery of joy, saying it was okay,
she knew she was worthless, she deserved this.
(*Come home, come home*, you cried. *Be well.*)

It was almost as though you loved her—
the way your heart stopped when she smiled
with only sorrow on her lips and walked away,
still not seeing she was beautiful, valuable.
(*Come home, come home*, you prayed. *Be loved.*)

HOPE

my God but we are all in
such desperate hope that
another will look us in the
eye and call us by name,
the name that summons
even the empty spaces,
and say to us, "You are
valued, just as you are,"
as though we have some
right to be on this earth,
breathing in hope like our
lungs can never be full enough

CURVED

I cannot breathe with your hands over my mouth
cramming the words back down my throat, still raw
from the days of swallowing the screams that my body
was not wrong, my heart was not broken. I am dying
under your weight on my chest as you tell me to stay
quiet, to keep my sins to myself so you don't have to
acknowledge that I cannot stop being what you deem
unnatural. I am gasping around this declaration stuck
in my mouth that I am not straight: I curve like a river,
a mountain chain weathered by storms, a thread holding
the clothing of my body together, a bird's flight in gales
of buffeting wind, a woman's hips to trace in wonder.
Nature does not abhor a curved line on this sphere
with a tilted axis and I do not know what to say to you
when you cover my mouth and insist on straight lines.

WHAT SHOULD WE CALL YOU?

They're not quite right, these lists of available pronouns
but I do not know to which department I should direct
my inquiry for more, I the glutton in abundance even
though we finally have more than two—three is enough,
recognizing that sexuality and gender are different is
enough, beggars can't be choosers. I am so tired of begging
for the chance to simply exist without being told I have
broken the rules with my self and some of these identifiers
are so close but not right, personalized keychains in kitschy
gift shops that never had my name but came close—one
syllable different, two, surely you can accept a nickname,
at least there's more than Jane and John. But I see what I
want in my mind on a placard and it is not on the list you
have given me and I remind myself I am not in the department
of pronoun acceptance; how can I read this many keychains
but still want another one, one tailored only to me, demanding
more as though I refuse to be kitsch named to others' specifications.

LABELED

You called me "queer" and I flinched from the punch
that you, a lesbian, did not mean to throw, this welcome
you intended of being One Of Us. I did not hear years
of homophobic slurs dripping bloodied from the vowel
in tripled barbed wire and baseball bats, slammed lockers
echoing down dangerously empty hallways of harsh
consonants, taunting sneers of the different outsiders.
I did not hear the implicit "freak" so many mean by it.
I heard a cage, an assumption, a meaning I do not know
how to apply to this body I cannot teach to be anything
other than itself, a freshly-starched shirt that pulls in
the shoulders and forces me to stand differently, a label
with expectations of who queer folk are supposed to be
but I have never tried to be this kind of person before
and I do not know how to be One Of You as simply me.

OVERHEARD

"Next they'll want to marry their dogs,"
says the knowing man to his chuckling friends
and I wonder if the queens of Stonewall will
forgive me for continuing to check my email,
for not interrupting to say I do not want to marry
my dog but to be in love with someone who
remembers my birthday even when I forget,
who smiles because I am alive with her, or him,
or whoever chases my heart and offers me theirs.
I wonder if the queens of Stonewall had days
when they could not fight the knowing man
and his chuckling friends who think love is not
part of marriage and marriage is not part of
humanity and humanity is anything other than
being seen as worthy of desire, relationship,
and hope that is a little out of reach for a dog.

CHRISTIAN

MOTIVATIONAL

A soft-edged photo of fog and growth told me,
"Sometimes when you're in a dark place, you think
you've been buried when actually you've been planted.

"Bloom."

It's a lovely thought and a beautiful fog, but I am not
a fucking daisy; I am determined. I will not wait quietly
in the dirt for the world to allow me water, sunlight, food,
life. I will not hope no one digs up my dark places before
I have roots that anchor me in life-giving shadow. I am
human, bold and brassy and tired of being told my grief
is a temporary necessity, my pain is a perfecting prelude.

I will not accept that something burying me is fine.

Blooming is an awakening over time that slowly fades; I
will erupt, not a flower but a fire that burns a path through
the darkness that is as real as death. Your soft edges have
no place in my sharp spirit because I have not been planted
but others have tried to bury me; I, like Jesus, am not yet
done and I, too, have some Hell-harrowing yet to do.

TWENTY-TWO

My Church, my Church, why have you forsaken me?
The baptismal waters still drip down my hair;
the oil's scent wafts down from my drying forehead.
Why have you cast me away from you? Why
have you looked at my journey and deemed it
less, wrong, twisted? I promised my faith when
you spoke my name in covenant; I pledged
that I would be loyal to you in seeking this God
who made us both. Is that not enough?
Why do you push me aside as though God cannot
love me, as though you cannot love me, as though I
cannot be loved? My Church, my Church, do not
throw me to the outer darkness—do not take
this family I have found, who has found me;
do not wrest me from these others who seek.
Hear, my Church: nothing—not texts nor speeches,
not tradition nor governance, not even you
can separate me from God's love in Christ Jesus.
What now shall we say to each other, Body?

WELCOMING

"When you get right down to it, we are all humans
with feelings," says the human whose feelings
are wounded enough to say this declaration
is too much, what if people knew we supported
this lifestyle unambiguously, surely we will lose
money, members, mission. When you get right
down to it, I cannot help but notice that your silence
only welcomes people like you, polite but noncommittal,
the ones who say my kind are welcome if we manage
to find your church with its statement of calculated
risk, its insistence that I offer myself on your altar
before I learn whether or not it is open to me.
"We are not anti-gay," you protest, horrified
to be lumped in with *those people* who are not
the lukewarm faithful spit out into parking lots,
those people who have not had a gay friend
like you have, from whom you didn't recoil even
once. But it's funny how there is so much space
between being anti-gay and being pro-inclusion,
a space as big as the lie you are telling that we are
all humans with feelings as though I do not feel
less when you tell me to accept these crumbs
for dogs who are allowed to be in this church if we
are quiet enough, hidden enough, not costing you
the members, mission, money whose feelings you value.

RELIGIONS

She told me of a god who frowned on her tears
and claimed weakness in the softening lines
of her bowed shoulders—"I don't want to be
a failure," she prayed to me, secret from this other.
Later I learned we had the same denomination
and my Buddhist friend (who is tired of Christians
telling him to come to a real God as though it's
a dating contest) laughed to see me so angry,
a vigilante minister railing that her god and my God
should be so totally different when our churches'
logos are the same. I told him better no Christ
than a fake one; he said that not many would prefer
that, but I do not see the difference between a god
who never met Israel and a god who frowns on
this broken woman's heart except that Brahma,
at least, seems to love her in her weary grief.

REPRIEVE

Today, you did not come for me.
Today, you did not stand in the public square and
tell the world that I am less, that I am evil, that I
am not as human or worthy or ethical as you think
you are, I should be. Today, you did not tell me to change.

Today, I am grateful for this.
Today, I am fully aware of the bullet I dodged whose
molten-hot jacket grazed my skin, burning a line
that will scar with a story only I know but at least
I can say that today I have not died from your shot.

Today, I am horrified by this.
Today, I am watching the people who did not survive
your other attempts to reroute the human heart by
starving it of love and hope and peace, the ones who
were dragged to the public square today to be killed.

Tomorrow, you might come for me.
Tomorrow, I am still not safe from your vindictiveness
that cries out for someone to flog on the scaffolding
of your theological certainty and it might be me because
I will still be wrong in your eyes when I am, tomorrow.

BOW

You say my kind has sullied the rainbow,
that you need to reclaim it from our sin-stained
fingers, that my pride is an affront to God's perfection
and I wonder if you realize that the rainbow is
an iWatch reminder to God not to commit genocide
when we break his heart again, and again, and again.
The first thing Noah did under this sign of hope
was get smash-down drunk in a cave—I would, too,
if the only people left were the family who'd stayed
in a floating zoo while the world died and I
had to figure out how to move thousands of
waterlogged corpses to plant crops. You say
my self is offensive to God as sin and I think
than when Ham uncovered his father's nakedness
everyone was a little bit hopeless because
the rainbow was a covenant no one felt
humanity could keep. You say you have to
reclaim the rainbow and I wonder if you know
it has always been a symbol of fierce defiance
against the idea that love or relationships
or the way we understand God is ever simple.

RELATABLE

Tell me again how you have walked my steps,
you who never had sex,
you who were born a man,
you who had Chrysostom's golden tongue
long before he did.

Tell me again how you, who reached a hand to lepers,
know what it is to flinch from touch, even yours—
especially yours—
in hands borrowed to rest in tears, to reassure,
to heal.

Tell me again, omniscient God,
human deity outmatching the half of Hercules,
what it is to be afraid.
That, you know.
You can tell that story.

Tell me, for the first time,
about your body no longer being yours
but man's;
about what it is to be shamed.
Tell me about being the means to someone else's end.

Tell me, King covered in a slave's scars,
how you were broken but are now alive—
for I would tell you of such things
and ask why I remain
dead.

PRAYERS

Maranatha—come, Holy Spirit, we sing,
arms flung to the sunless rafters,
voices swallowed by the cavernous maw
in which we dare call ourselves the Body of Christ.

Maranatha—come, Holy Spirit, we sing,
arms slinging the paperwork we pile to Heaven
as though Babel could be re-legislated if God
would only hear our point of order, paragraph number.

Maranatha—come, Holy Spirit, we sing,
arms crossed over closed hearts that shout
the Spirit may come but not her children;
fire that doesn't burn too hot, water that is dry.

Maranatha—come, Holy Spirit, we sing,
arms holding our fear that God will listen,
breaking through our ideas of what we know
Jesus meant when he said, "I love you."

Maranatha—come, Holy Spirit, we whisper,
arms forced open by the weight of this millstone
we have given each other, one certainty at a time,
necks broken on the gallows we made for someone else.

Maranatha—come, Holy Spirit, we choke,
arms numb from the poison in our mouths
from the cup of blood we no longer believe will save
this Church that calls for a Spirit we do not know.

INCOMPATIBILITY

It is not about whether I am incompatible
with the teachings of this crafted faith that hopes
to name the unnamable, to see the Wind itself,
to call to the One who created the bodies we wear.
It is about whether I am incompatible with
you, the holy human brandishing a thrice-turned
textual god whose salvation comes by prepositions
and whose grace never comes at all.
It is about whether I am incompatible with
the concept of divine love that dances in the waves
of a handsome woman's hipbones, a beautiful man's hair,
a laugh that comes out of a moment unmarried to sex.
It is about whether I am incompatible with
electricity, male plug to female outlet, genderless sparks
flying from this centuries-old abomination that brought light
to a world of candles, stars, crackling bonfires, lovers' pens.
It is about whether you are incompatible with
me, whose name you will not say, whose self you claim
is incompatible with the teaching but not the God
who taught us that love means dying before resurrection.

UNTHREATENING

To the sidewalk preachers, Bible thumpers,
purity police, and defenders of God's goodness:

You tell me I cannot stand before God as
a sexual deviant, an abomination, a sinner.

Amateurs.

You bring the threat of hellfire and damnation
as though I have not already burned myself alive,

each day a new way to peel the shame out of me,
cutting the flesh that never stops healing,

a Sisyphean ecstasy of the Hell I accepted
that damns more thoroughly than your poster-board.

You bring the threat of Scriptures calling my "kind" evil
as though I have not memorized them in several languages,

carving the words into the body I cannot redirect,
branding them on the heart that still insists on loving.

You bring no threat, you whitewashed tombs, no damnation
because you cannot frighten me or hurt me more than

I have already hurt and frightened myself. Amateurs,
sons and daughters of the selfsame Adam who took

the fruit from the beautiful woman from the beautiful snake
because we have all fallen short of the glory of God

and you cannot kill me any faster than my own slow suicide
that started long before you and your two-bit crusade.

If you had any idea of what hellfire really felt like,
sister sinner, brother broken, you would not threaten me

but bandage the wounds I inflicted with the hands of the thieves
who came before you, taking even my clothes; you would care

as though you were my neighbor, sorrowing over a traveler's pain,
both of us in desperate need of the coolness of the baptismal waters.

MORE

"You are more than this role for which you are paid,"
says the soft voice meant to be comforting, meant
to call me back to the integrated body where the eye
and the foot do not say they are self-sufficient.
"You are more than this title by which we call you,"
says the gentle voice meant to be soothing, meant
to assure me that God looked at everything that was
created and said yes, this is so very good, beloved.
I am more than this calling to which I have agreed
say I to the voice meant to be reassuring, meant
to allow me to be, but you have also told me my "more"
is too much, not enough, and my dis-integration breaks
the gentle reassurance because I cannot be all with you.

SPLIT

I heard you were leaving for good, had it planned,
complete with new name and new kicks and old
habits of exclusion but let bygones be bygones, no
hard feelings—this thing between us just couldn't last.
You cowardly, duplicitous, self-serving serpent, you
wolf among sheep, how dare you tell me to be civil.
You want me to say good riddance to our poisonous
divorce but it was you who closed every loophole, you
who swore that no house of God would be thus polluted
by false leaders like me, you who took the barbs of a book
called discipline to break the spine of the unruly beloved.
You sliced an autopsy's y-cut into the chest of the Body
of Christ and now, now when it dares to bleed instead of
staying dead in the grave you loaned, you want to leave.
A website will be announced with a logo that probably
won't include a symbolic kiss but I see you anyway, Judas,
and I stand in the garden knowing that death comes before
resurrection and that I will still not draw my sword here.
You have heard that I am incompatible with Christian teachings
but I tell you that Christ taught about millstones and fire
and I cannot even begin to understand how you can justify
standing in the pulpit to proclaim love while the Body bleeds
no matter what logo shines on the screen behind you.

FOR SHAME

"I will never see you as shameful,"
says the God who was crucified naked,
bloodied and pinned, presented to the mother
weeping as death took the life she'd borne.
"But," I say, I always say, as though
I have ever wanted to hear anything
as much as these words, "but see what I
have *done*, who I have *become*, this broken thing."
The God who made aardvarks and jellyfish
and loves the Venus flytrap shrugs.

"I will never see you as shameful,"
says the God who wore a circlet of thorns,
his friends denying knowing him in fear
of being caught, in horror of being wrong.
"But," I whisper, sometimes shout as though
if I am loud enough I will win this loss,
"but hear what I have *said*, how I have *lied*
about you and me to the world."
The God who made Jupiter and the Orien Nebula
and loves the creatures from two galaxies over sighs.

"I will never see you as shameful,"
says this God who hears my inmost self
pierced by my accusations and delighted by
my joy in simply becoming, one breath at a time.
"*Oh*," I say, I only say because there is nothing
else on my tongue in the face of the love that is,
was, has yet to be, "oh, see what I am being loved into."
The God who made the atom and the evening
and loves me, all of me as myself, smiles.

HOLINESS

"It is because the Lord demands holiness,"
soothes the gentle explanation of why my heart
cannot coexist with my soul this side of Hell
and I appreciate the concern for purity here
in this post-Paul pocket beyond the Law, but
I sat in an unyielding pew beside a man who
lusted after a woman but still had both his eyes;
a woman whose ex-husband had not died when
her current husband wished him happy birthday;
a pastor's father who lied to a child about God
watching to ensure she ate all her broccoli without
being buried under a millstone at the bottom of
the sea—so forgive me if I begin to wonder whether
you are less concerned with holiness and purity
than with your disgust at my girlfriend's affection.

RELIGION

They said I wasn't welcome there
beneath the frowning cross.
I had too many sins to bear;
my gain would be their loss.
They said to try on down the street
at churches less like theirs—
those were the ones where sinners meet
and voice to God their prayers.

Gimme that old-time religion;
gimme that never-was religion;
gimme that could-it-be religion
where hope is given free.

The open doors and open hands
were closed in love's pure name;
the gay and bi and queer and trans
were told we were to blame.
The evil wasn't us, per se;
it was the sin inside
but since we'd led ourselves astray
from God, we couldn't hide.

Gimme that old-time religion;
gimme that all-have-sinned religion;
gimme that loved-the-world religion
where grace is given free.

But I can tell you, one to one,
there're other words from God;
this faith they say that we've undone
is nothing but a fraud.
Beloved one, it is no sin
to be loved and to love—

in fact, that's how each day begins
in gift from Heaven above.

So gimme that old-time religion;
gimme that Jesus-led religion;
gimme that made-to-last religion
where love is given free.

Part Two

LITURGY

SERVICE WITH COMMUNION

SETTING THE SYMBOLS

Worship is a multisensory experience and being deliberate about engaging those senses is a helpful way to invite worshippers to be fully present. This service is written as though the worshipping body is together in person but can be adapted to virtual worship if needed.

The visual aspect is often a good starting point and while rainbows are an easy symbol of inclusion in the faith conversation, I challenge worship planners to get creative with how that is presented. Is it just a picture of a rainbow or are there multiple colors of fabric entwined with each other? Several heights and colors of candles or statues of different types and colors of human figures could also speak to diversity and inclusion. The wild variety of creation itself is a good alternative or companion to the rainbow; many types of flowers or vines give richness and depth to the visual scene and could be adapted to the tactile and scent aspects of the service by giving each worshipper a petal of a silk flower or a leaf (be careful if using real plants in case of participant allergies).

You know your worship setting best for types of music and where hymns or songs fit best in your service, so I have not put hymns in this service order. Feel free to experiment with different kinds of music and invite people into songleading who may not have done so before but are willing to try.

LITURGY

Call to Worship

We come to worship as we are, carrying worries and fears.
You are already listening to what we bear, God of easy burdens.
We come to worship as we are, seeking healing and strength.
You are already willing to soothe, God of wholeness.

We come to worship as we are, rejoicing in hope and wonder.
We bring all of ourselves, God of all things, to be present with you.

Collect

Creator and creative God who delights in the wonderous diversity of all
that you have made, open our hearts to the new ways in which you are
continually teaching us to see your world. Grant us the strength to follow
the ways you lead that may not be familiar to us, recognizing that you invite
us to wholeness in all things by your healing name. Amen.

Prayer for illumination

Create in us willing hearts, God who is still speaking, to hear the ways in
which you tell us who you are and who we are becoming as your people in
the word that guides the journey of faith.

SCRIPTURE

Many services use a psalm offered as a gathering script after a prayer of
illumination as separate from the preaching text. Especially in a service of
inclusion, the more Scripture the better to show that God's word is not only
welcome but necessary as part of worship. United Methodist, Episcopal,
and Presbyterian (USA) hymnals all have responsive settings of most of the
psalms, or it can be read by one or several people helping to lead worship.
Suggested psalms include 4, 11, 13, 22, 27, 40, 42, 56, 57, 86, 121, 130, 139,
or 146.

An important part of any sermon or homily in an LGBTQ+ inclusive
service is the recognition that Scripture has been used over and over again
to cause harm in the form of alienation and judgment. The introduction of
the preaching texts should acknowledge this and name the fact that Scrip-
ture is not and should never be a weapon before going on to unpack a text
that is healing.

Suggested sermon texts include Genesis 1 and God's decree that all
creation is good; 2 Samuel 1 and the close relationship between Jonathan
and David that brought them both joy; Psalm 139 and the reality that God
knows us and cares for all of who we are; Matthew 25 and the reality that it

is our care for each other that defines us rather than any gender or sexuality conformation; John 6 and the declaration by Jesus that all are under his care and entrusted to him; Acts 8 and the reality that those who stand outside the "accepted" structures have always been welcome as the eunuch was; Romans 8 and the reassurance that nothing can separate us from God's love; 1 Corinthians 12 and the call for all of the parts of the Body to work in concert with the gifts God has given; or 1 Corinthians 13 and the call for love to undergird all that we do.

COMMUNION

Invitation to Communion

1: The One we call Christ invites all to this table,

2: all who love the neighbor made in God's image,

1: all who love the God who created so much more than us,

2: all who seek to repent of the ways we mar that creation.

1: Come, let us confess before God and one another.

2: Let us confess the part we play in our imperfect world. Let us pray.

Prayer of Confession

**God of infinite diversity, God of holy mystery, God of boundless love, we come to you as the breaker and the broken.
We repent of the sorrow that we have let fester into rage;
we repent of the fear that we have let grow into faithlessness;
we repent of the grief that we have let spin into despair.
Forgive us, Spirit of mercy, for the moments when we look at this world and forget to see your grace. Forgive us when we speak for you out of our own worry.
Turn our sorrow into wisdom, our fear into faith, our grief into hope.
Remake us, Anointed One, even as you remind us that your love is unfailing, unflinching, unafraid of anything we hold in our secret hearts.**

61

Show us how to bring the mercy you so freely give to everyone in this world who longs for good news, for a reason to hope.
Free us for your work of restoration through Jesus the Christ, firstborn over all creation, as we continue to pray...

(All pray in silence; I've found that having a full 60 seconds both makes people uncomfortable and gives them the chance to center in the ritual.)

In the name of the Life-giver, **Amen.**

Pardon

1: Hear this good news:

2: Before we even thought to ask, God's love bound Godself in relationship with us.

1: Through the death and resurrection of Jesus Christ, we are made whole.

2: In the name of Jesus Christ, you are forgiven.

In the name of Jesus Christ, you are forgiven.
Glory to God! Amen.

The Peace

As people reconciled to the Holy One, forgiven by the God of justice, and called by name to this community of beloved disciples, let us turn to each other as siblings in the family of God, offering signs of peace.

The Eucharistic Prayer

May God be with you.
And also with you.
Let us lift up our hearts.
We lift them up to the Lord.
Let us give thanks to our Creator God.
It is right and healing to offer our thanks and praise.

1: It is right, and a good and joyful thing, always and everywhere to give thanks to you, holy and inviting Spirit. In the formless dark before time itself you saw what could be and spoke light into the universe, bringing creation into being.

2: You molded us from the mud and breathed life into us, delighting in the difference of more than one human displaying your vast wonder.

1: When we took your breath of life and used it for death, you remained beside us, steadfast through every time we told ourselves that you had left.

2: Through the prophets, the kings, the murderers, the thieves, the adulterers, the judges, the warriors, the faithful, and the faithless, you saw what could be and spoke light into our darkness.

1: When you became human yourself and lived into our pain and our frailty, still you called us by name, reminding us that we are beloved.

2: In awe and humility we join our hearts and voices with your people on earth and the vast cloud of witnesses in Heaven, saying,

Holy, holy, holy Lord, God of mercy and light, heaven and earth are full of your glory.
Hosanna in the highest!
Blessed is the One who comes in the name of the Lord.
Hosanna in the highest!

1: Holy are you and blessed is your child Jesus Christ. In the waters of the Spirit you anointed him as your beloved to preach good news to the poor and bring freedom to the captives, to liberate the oppressed, heal the broken, and feed the hungry.

2: You ate with those others deemed unworthy, announcing the deliverance of *all* people. From the sorrow of the cross you brought life abundant, giving birth to your church and making with us a new covenant by water and the Spirit.

1: Gathered once more around your table, we remember. On the night in which He was betrayed by the friends who had called him teacher, Jesus took the bread of the meal, gave thanks to you, blessed the bread, and broke it. He gave it to the disciples, saying, "Take, and eat. This is my body, given for you. Do this in remembrance of me."

2: After the supper, Jesus took the cup and said, "Take, and drink. This is my blood of the new covenant, poured out for you and for many for the forgiveness of sins. Do this, as often as you drink it, in remembrance of me."

1: And so, in remembrance of the mighty wonder of making the ordinary extraordinary, we take bread and cup, offering ourselves in praise and gratitude for this divine gift offered freely to the whole world. In the power of your faithfulness and the joy of our redemption we proclaim the mystery of faith:

Christ has died. Christ is risen! Christ will come again.

2: Send your life-giving breath upon us gathered here and on these remembrances of bread and juice, that in sharing in these we might share in the life of Christ and be the Body to a waiting world. As we are united in Christ, may your Spirit unite us in faith that in all things we might grow in love and grace as disciples of the Hope of the world. **Amen.**

As we come to the table that is open to all, let us pray with the confidence of the children of God:
Nurturing One in whom Heaven dwells,
may your name be made holy.
May your kingdom be brought to our lives,
may your will be our way
that earth may mirror the justice of the heavens.
Give us enough to sustain us today,
and forgive us our sins,
even as we forgive those who sin against us.
Do not let us fall to temptation,
but deliver us from evil.
For yours are the kingdom, the power, and the glory eternal. Amen.

The Meal

Prayer after Receiving

God of reckless and unbounded love, we give you thanks for this holy mystery in which you have given yourself to us, flinging wide the invitation that all your creation may be fed. Send us forth as your people,

welcomed and loved, that we may bring your invitation to those who feel shut out. By the guidance of your Spirit, may we offer ourselves as salt and light, steadfast in faith and generous in mercy, until we come again to your feast of more than we can imagine. Amen.

Benediction

CREATING YOUR OWN LITURGY

WHEN WRITING LITURGY, don't try to start from scratch; you stand on thousands of years of church history. Use it. If you belong to a particular denomination, see what patterns of service order they have—hymnals are a great resource for this. Just like poetry, reading liturgy can help open your own liturgical voice because you get a sense of the possible rhythm.

The backbone of liturgy is prayer, which may be frightening to some people. There are several jokes about the fastest way to silence a church meeting being asking for someone to pray, and it's true. Very few people feel comfortable with public prayer for all sorts of reasons. When the tension of sexuality and faith is introduced, the discomfort level may rise astronomically—what if I say the wrong thing? What if I misname something?

The important thing to remember about prayer is that it is a conversation between you and God to which other people are listening in, not an address to other people on which God is eavesdropping, so begin with a comfortable title. Do you love the idea of Creator God? Hate parental language? Always begin thinking about God via the human incarnation of Jesus? Start there; don't use "father" or "mother" if you don't feel connected to God with that, and do use "Holy One" or "Spirit of life" if that is how you recognize that you're stepping into awareness of God's constant presence.

When the disciples asked Jesus how to pray, Jesus gave them what has become a ritual but was meant as a template. The Lord's Prayer is a beautiful resource and if you want to include it in your liturgy that is great, but the rhythm of it is helpful even without the familiar words: address, praise, request, praise. A prayer can be as simple as, "God, you are great; help me to see that, by the wondrous nature of your name. Amen." Or it can be as complex as you need. Let yourself experiment with what you're creating in offering to God with this service as you're writing opening prayers, congregational concerns, and closing responses.

If you'd like to use one of the poems in this book to help shape liturgy, decide whether you want it to be read by worship leaders, as a call-and-response piece with the congregation, or said by the congregation as a whole.

The shorter poems better lend themselves to use in a worship service unless they are a key component of a sermon or longer piece of meditation, and feel free to borrow from them for use as a springboard as needed. For example, "A Little Bit Free" can be adapted to a Sunday morning call to worship like this:

But tonight I dance with broken feet and feel the music's sway— tonight I challenge all to meet the fierceness of my way. Tonight I fling my arms out wide and exhale to the sky; tonight I'm on my own damn side and refuse your caging "why."	This morning, we dance on broken feet **and yet we feel your music's sway.** This morning, we challenge ourselves, **gathering in the fierceness of the Spirit.** This morning, we fling our arms open, **exhaling the ways others hold us back.** This morning, we celebrate in worship, **trusting the limitless One who calls us.**

In a service of affirmation and inclusion, you may wish to include a creed. There are several in the history of the church that you can use outright or as a starting point, such as the Apostles' Creed and the Nicene Creed. There are also social creeds that came out of the Social Gospel movement of the early 20th century that are closer to the issues with which we wrestle today. The United Methodist social creed is toward the front of the *Book of Discipline*—yes, the same book that is so deftly used to exclude queer people—and also on the UMC website under "What We Believe." The National Council of Churches has written a "21st Century Social Creed" that is on their website (NationalCouncilOfChurches.us).

The other main piece of liturgy is confession and assurance. I encourage you to incorporate this if you are doing a service of inclusion and support because inclusion without recognition of harm is shallow at best. Confessions should be general enough to be applicable to an entire congregation but specific enough that they are real confessions. This can be a tricky balance; a useful framework is to go "from the outside in": world–nation/denomination–neighborhood/church–personal relationships–self. You don't have to include all of these (and many do not), but an example of all of them would be something like this:

> Lord, too often we forget that you are God of all things. Forgive us our neglect of our siblings who are still fighting in other countries to be recognized as full human beings; show us how to recognize the ways in which people are excluded for who they are in the church spaces we uphold and call home; open the eyes of our hearts to see those we profess to love who feel unheard and

unsupported by us; and have mercy on us for the ways in which we deny our own multiplicity of identities to fit ourselves into someone else's status quo.

It is *vital* that any confession be followed by reassurance; we do not confess to inform God that we are terrible people but so that we can recognize the magnitude of God's grace and love as the relationship continues.

If you'd like to go deeper in the nuts and bolts of writing liturgy, there are some resources about the process under "Faith" in Appendix A.

To you, Lord, be the glory;
to you, Lord, be the pain;
to you, Lord, be the joy, and
to you, Lord, be the rain.

To you, Lord, be the snowfall;
to you, Lord, be the night;
to you, Lord, be my soul-self
for shelter in your light.

Part Three

WORKSHOP

Option One: Short Book Study

This is designed to be used in person, virtually, or as a hybrid option as an hour-and-a-half one-time session. The COVID-19 pandemic has irreversibly altered the way we approach small group gatherings and its effects will not go away anytime soon, so peppered throughout this study guide are suggestions for how to tailor the questions to virtual or in-person communication. Where two or more are gathered in God's name, there Christ is, and sometimes that gathering is much more geographically broad than we had previously imagined.

Opening (25 minutes)

(Up to ten minutes): Even if the group is relatively familiar with itself, have participants introduce themselves by name, pronouns, and what they bring to this study in terms of experience with poetry. If you are using a virtual gathering format, this can be a good way to learn muting/unmuting techniques and to check that anyone calling in can hear everyone clearly. Make it clear that pronouns are an optional part of identification—it can be as damaging to force someone to self-identify as to assume their identity in the first place. Keep this brief; it is laying groundwork, not building profiles.

(Five minutes): After introductions, lead a centering moment. This is not the same as an opening prayer; that may feel right for your session, but so much of this topic is charged with religion-based trauma that I recommend easing into it.

A centering moment is not necessarily religious but is a deliberate choice to be in this place and no other. If you have a favorite, short practice, use that. If not, try this: have the group steeple their fingers together. Ask them to consider the pressure of their fingertips as gravity pushes on their bodies; the temperature of their hands; whether or not they can feel their pulse. Tell the group to breathe deeply. Encourage them to take the concerns and joys of the day and fit them into the space their hands have created. Breathe deeply. Instruct the group to offer all that is in that space to God, knowing that they can take it back after this session if they really want to but for right now, what is outside the room is God's and they do not have to carry it. Direct them to open their hands if that helps the visualization, or rest that space on a table to tell themselves they are setting it down. Breathe deeply. Explain that now we are present to this time, giving ourselves permission to be here and nowhere else.

You may wish to make explicit, before or after the centering moment, what that presence looks like. Encourage participants to silence their cell phones; if you are meeting virtually, invite them to close all other tabs and programs on their devices so they can focus on this. The lack of interruption and shifting is as much in respect for the others in the group as we explore together.

(Ten minutes): Because the conversations around identity and faith cannot help but be fraught with emotion and personal connection, create a group covenant. It does not have to be in-depth, but set the expectations of confidentiality, engaged listening, respect and accountability, and holding space for disagreement versus tolerating bigotry. Make sure the group accepts the covenant with clear verbal agreement before proceeding. If you're meeting virtually, have someone type the basic tenets in the chat box so people can refer to it as needed.

Study (40 minutes)

With creativity, we learn by doing. Choose two poems from this collection beforehand to act as examples. If the group is larger than ten people, consider having a second leader so there can be two groups (in virtual format, this can be randomly assigned breakout or chat rooms). Have two people read the poem; try to have them be two different genders, if possible. Leave a minute in between the readings for people to process. After the readings, start questions at the general level. What stuck out to the listeners? Why?

Once there is some comfort in responding, allow the conversation to become more specific. (As the leader, do not be afraid of silence; some people may take time to process this and gather the courage to be honest. Refrain from filling silences immediately, even though they may be uncomfortable.) Was there any part that resonated with them personally? Were there parts that they would rework or rewrite? What? Are there other poems or works they know of which the poem reminded them? Are there any Scriptures of which this reminds them or with which they would put this in conversation? Be careful not to let any participant become a guest lecturer who takes up the conversational space to talk about this as an academic topic only. Keep the group covenant close to hand to support how you're guiding the experience.

Break (5 minutes)

Discuss (15 minutes)

If the group has split, come back together for the closing conversation and have a spokesperson summarize what the groups discussed. Return to the things that were said in the introductions of what experience with poetry people said they had. Are there people who have written their own? Have they written with faith in mind? If so, how did that change the writing process? If someone hasn't read poetry for a long time, what was it like to come back to it now?

Scripture is itself poetry in many parts (read a short psalm if there is time). How does it change participants' understanding of holy texts to think of them as poetry as well as prose? What do the two media do differently as means of communication?

Choose beforehand a line from one of the poems in this collection that strikes you and present it to the group as a writing challenge. If there is an opportunity for the group to keep in contact, encourage people to share their creations later as they are comfortable. From that one line (which can go anywhere in their poem), invite participants to write their own work on faith and identity. It can be any structure or none at all but it must use that line; this gives a starting point to those who may not be familiar with poetry as a faith exercise.

Benediction (10 minutes)

Ask if there are any questions about the process or need for further discussion. Be mindful that the topics of faith, gender, and sexuality can stir some powerful things in people and that there may be people who need space to deal with their reactions. As the leader, know and respect your own limits;

if someone has questions or reactions that are beyond your ability to handle, refer them to a pastor, therapist, or other professional for longer-term conversation. Close with a benediction—Iona Abbey has several books of liturgy with pieces that are well-suited to identity exploration, or you can make your own or use another of the poems from this book. Thank participants for their time and their honesty in involvement.

Option Two: Creative Workshop

WHETHER YOU DO THIS virtually or in-person, this four-hour-long workshop will need to have breaks built in so that your participants do not meld to their chairs. Decide ahead of time whether they should be every half hour, every hour, or every two hours and vary the type of break—five minute stand-and-stretch breaks can be more frequent, 15-minute walk-around-and-absorb-information breaks less so. C.S. Lewis once said that, "In poetry, words are the body"—don't ask your participants to forget theirs.

The nature of a longer workshop isn't substantially different than the shorter, one-time group study, but the main addition is the ability to work through one's own poetry. This is not intended to be a conference panel but an interactive invitation to create from participants' understanding of sexuality and faith. Read through the section on the Short Book Study for guidelines about introductions and creating a group covenant, recognizing that the longer format can allow for more time on questions like "what brought you here" or deeper collaboration on the group covenant.

Opening (30 minutes)

Beginning with a prayer or other mindfulness practice helps set the tone for the day as a place of spiritual exploration that does not expect doctrinal perfection. If you as the leader do not wish to lead this, speak with someone a few days before the workshop so that they have time to prepare something appropriate.

After the prayer, set the expectations: if the workshop is virtual or hybrid, run through etiquette notes of muting, raising hands, chatting, and so on. Let people know if you require them to have their cameras on for the duration or if they can turn them off when they need to be less "on." If the workshop is only in person, remind people of where restrooms are, whether there are refreshments, whether they are allowed to get up and move around if needed, and how you as the leader will operate in terms of facilitating but not forcing participation.

Take the time to work with the group to create a covenant for the day. It does not have to be in-depth, but set the rules of confidentiality, engaged listening, respect and accountability, and holding space for disagreement versus tolerating bigotry. Make sure the group accepts the covenant with clear verbal agreement before proceeding. If you're meeting virtually, have someone type the basic tenets in the chat box so people can refer to it as needed.

Teaching (40 minutes)

There are three categories of things that matter most in poetry (and, perhaps, in theology): form, rhythm, and imagery.

Form includes the important questions of how we begin and end poetry. This is the nuts and bolts of writing poetry and includes the use (or deliberate misuse) of grammar, the intentionality of line breaks, the look of it (is it a shape poem?), and the rules by which the poem plays. Ask participants what kinds of poems they already know; many will likely think of couplets (aa bb cc dd and so on) or short sonnets. Some may think of the poet ee cummings and the refusal to capitalize anything. For the kinetic poets among us, talk about form as the things you consider if you were to build a poem. Would it look more like the Taj Mahal with lots of fancy phrases broken smartly across lines and punctuation making all sorts of statements, or more like the Empire State Building with a bang at the top but not much excitement until the end?

Rhythm is the extension of form and deals with the writing flow. This is the time to consider things like meter, rhyme scheme, onomatopoeia, consonance, and assonance. If a person wants to write a particular form of poem, such as a sonnet or a villanelle rather than free form or a limerick, the rhythm will differ according to the rules of that form. Have your poets think through pleasing speeches and the ways words play off of each other in various examples. (Use some of the poets from the Poetry section in Appendix B as illustrations. slats is a good poet for examining use of form while Emily Dickenson is a prime example of the particular use of rhythm—her poems fit the meter of "Gilligan's Island," which some of your poets may already know.)

Imagery is where the difference between poetry and prose packs a punch. Because poetry is (usually) short, there isn't a lot of space in which to develop the image the poet is wishing to convey. From whose point of view are we seeing the image or action of the poem? What is the scene itself? Is the image meant to be emotionally evocative? If so, how? If poets are unsure where to begin, have them list descriptive words as a group—the more obscure, the better. Does "cloudy" land differently than "overcast"? Why?

In this section, remind people that poetry has a lot of forms and a lot of voices; it's not only okay but important that each writer try their own form and their own voices and see where it leads.

Discussing (60 minutes)

This section and the teaching section may bleed into each other, time-wise, which is fine. You as the leader know your people best. This is a time when people get to celebrate what they already know and what they may never have heard about—someone may know that sonnets should be 14 lines, for example, but may not know that there are at least three recognized forms.

Encourage people to ask questions and have several books of poetry along so that people can dig into the work of others as foundations on which to build their own explorations. Use the poems here to talk about what works and what doesn't in terms of form, rhythm, and imagery. Have the group work together (if there are more than 12 people, split into two) and take on a poem from this book to rewrite in a new form, or to focus on a different image than the one presented.

It is not necessary for you as the leader to be an expert poet in order to lead this discussion, though it may help if you brush up on some poetic terms beforehand (see the list under "Poetry" in Appendix A). This time is about people bringing in their own existing knowledge and putting shared language around the craft of poetry.

Writing (30 minutes)

Armed with curiosity, knowledge, and a bit of group practice, it is time for the poets to go write for themselves. It can help to give a single line around which people can build their poem—for example, "because you were asleep and I wanted nothing" from "Late Night." Instruct your writers to use that somewhere in their poem; or, if you feel they are comfortable, simply let them go without a prompt at all.

Where one writes can be almost as important as *what* one writes, as very few of us can comfortably delve into our poetic selves seated at a table like school. Have set places people can wander to write, whether other rooms in the building or places outside they can curl up and think. Encourage them to note their setting if they feel stuck for a poem, incorporating a color or a sound into their exploration of faith and identity. Building off of verses of Scripture can also be a useful starting point, especially if there is some wrestling to be done with the text.

Remind your participants to be kind to themselves. Poetry can become an intense emotional outlet, and while there is nothing wrong with that in itself, a workshop is not a therapy session. If they need to pause or walk around or whatever, they are welcome to do so. They can write as many poems in the half hour as they like, but set the expectation that there will be one they are willing to bring back to the group.

Sharing (40 minutes)

Have the group return, stretch, and shake themselves out for this part—this is vulnerability in spades and it has taken the group hours to get to being able to do this. Restate the group covenant to remind everyone that constructive feedback is welcome but destructive criticism is not. Remind everyone that they will have to read something, but it does not have to be the deepest thing they've written. Reassure them that they have written poetry—whether it is "good" is less important than that it *is*—which means they are now all poets and can claim the name even if this is the first poem they've ever written. Whether their poem is award-worthy or not, it is a poem and they are a poet and that matters.

Start with a volunteer (whom you may wish to ask to lead beforehand) and begin the process of reading, acknowledging, giving feedback, and being thankful for that person's poem. The person can either read their own poem or ask someone else to read it. It is customary at poetry read-ings to snap rather than clapping after a reading, which may or may not be a method of acknowledgment that you wish to use. Invite the rest of the group to note what they heard in form, rhythm, and imagery, asking ques-tions respectfully as needed. Thank the poet after the time of feedback for writing the work, sharing the work, and listening to others' views.

You as the leader need to be part of this, so take the half hour before to write at least one poem of your own. This creates trust and erodes distance in this exploration of identity; be aware that the rules of meriting respect, being a poet, and listening courteously also apply to you.

Closing (10 minutes)

After everyone has read, thank everyone again for attending and engaging this. Any follow-up notes go here, if applicable. Have a benediction chosen beforehand, create one out of the experiences of the day, or use the prayer at the end of "Creating Your Own Liturgy" to send your poets on their way. Be sure to know your own limits for whether you can stay after to talk with people about anything that was unearthed in the process of writing and have resources of other people with whom they can talk if you cannot be that person.

Appendix A

RESOURCES

THIS ANNOTATED BIBLIOGRAPHY IS by no means meant to be exhaustive of the ways people discuss faith and sexuality. It is a first step. You may already be familiar with many of the volumes listed here; the bibliographies in each of these books is a further step. I also encourage you to learn through conversation—not in the sense of asking someone on the rainbow to explain everything, but in the sense of being curious with people you trust who may be able to give you other resources for information and experience.

FAITH

The Book of Discipline of The United Methodist Church 2016. Nashville, TN: United Methodist Publishing House, 2016.

Though this is not a beach read, it is a UMC-specific resource for how this denomination thinks about itself. It is the handbook of how to be a Methodist and includes everything from the history of the denomination to the number of committees required in a local church. The language against homosexuality is here—but so is a beautiful opening section called the Social Principles that details religious understandings of sexuality, abortion, ecological capitalism, animal cruelty, and so much more. It is a book that has been structured and restructured by committee over more than fifty years, so it is a bit of a labyrinth but is a helpful tool if you're trying to understand the structure and politics of the UMC. The Presbyterian Church (USA) has an equivalent in the *Book of Order*; for beliefs rather than organizational structures, see the *Book of Concord* for the Evangelical Lutheran Church in America (ELCA) or the *Book of Common Prayer* for the Episcopal Church.

Cantorna, Amber. *Unashamed: A Coming-Out Guide for LGBTQ Christians*. Louisville, KY: Westminster John Knox Press, 2019.

This gentle guide starts from the very basics of grappling with internalized homophobia and working toward self-acceptance before progressing to acceptance in one's social and professional spheres. It also assumes a connection to more conservative and unsupportive Christianity in its reader. Even if these beginning points do not apply, the reassurance and bedrock hope grounded in Scriptural declarations of love and goodness are a boon to anyone navigating coming out in their community of faith.

Cheng, Patrick S. *Radical Love: An Introduction to Queer Theology*. New York: Seabury Books, 2011.

Rev. Dr. Cheng's overview of queer theology joins the ranks of contextual theologies such as Black theology, feminist theology, Latin American liberation theologies, and several other viewpoint-specific examinations by historically marginalized voices. This book acts as a historical survey as well as a general introduction to the ways in which queer theology can be applied in the modern age. While written with scholastic efforts in mind, it is fairly accessible in its language.

Cherry, Kittredge and Zalmon Sherwood, eds. *Equal Rites: Lesbian and Gay Worship, Ceremonies, and Celebrations*. Louisville, KY: Westminster John Knox Press, 1995.

For those of us with the charge of creating worship, this book is a good resource for the language of important moments. The examples work ecumenically and include the regular church ceremonies like baptism, communion, funerals, and weddings. They also address the focused worship needs of the LGBTQ+ community with liturgies for coming out, recovering from assault, celebrating Pride, and rediscovering family. Some of the more recent books of worship within the major denominations have included such liturgies, but this is a good place to start for how wide a range inclusive liturgy can and should take.

Jennings, Jr., Theodore W. "Breaking Down the Walls of Division: Challenges Facing the People Called Methodist." In *Methodist and Radical: Rejuvenating a Tradition*, edited by Joerg Rieger and John J. Vincent, 53–65. Nashville, TN: Kingswood Books, 2003.

Jennings looks very specifically at The United Methodist Church and the ways our denominational disagreement over the inclusion of all sexualities has hindered our mission and vision as a part of the Body of Christ. He suggests several ways in which we must open the denomination if we are to move forward in spiritual health. Given that this was written well before the 2019 General Conference, some of the information is a bit dated. It is, however, still a good resource for those within the UMC pondering what is next.

Job, Rueben P. and Neil M. Alexander, eds. *Finding Our Way: Love and Law in The United Methodist Church*. Nashville, TN: Abingdon Press, 2014.

This is a decent (if dated) and quick overview of the positions within the UMC and how the Church has never dealt with its own uncertainties around sexual identity in any holistic sense. For those new to the denominational struggle or for those looking for just how many viewpoints there are, this is a good starting point that strives to present the sides without clearly advocating for one.

Knust, Jennifer Wright. *Unprotected Texts: The Bible's Surprising Contradictions about Sex and Desire*. New York: HarperOne, 2011.

While Knust's overview does not focus exclusively on the ways in which Scripture has been read against LGBTQ+ inclusion, it does include the recognition alongside examinations of prescribed gender roles and sex outside of heterosexual marriage. Knust's aim is not so much to "prove" one interpretation or another as to showcase the reality that our modern interpretations miss the original context of Scriptural sexual culture. This is helpful for those who are looking to dig into the textual complexities of sexuality in general.

Oliveto, Karen P. *Our Strangely Warmed Hearts: Coming out into God's Call.* Nashville, TN: Abingdon Press, 2018.

As the first openly lesbian bishop in The United Methodist Church, Oliveto has the lens and the experience to discuss the ways in which sexuality and faith weave into each other. This survey of stories and real experiences from those living in the tension and wonder of sexuality and faith begins with a short primer on LGBTQ+ history in the United States. It continues with a specifically Wesleyan lens to call for not only inclusion but celebration of all the people God invites into ministry.

Robertson, Brandan. *True Inclusion: Creating Communities of Radical Embrace.* St. Louis, MO: Chalice Press, 2018.

If you are reading my poems and planning to do either of the workshops, chances are that your organization is trying to be or already considers itself inclusive. But is it fully living into inclusivity or are there still habits and patterns that hold some people at arm's length? Robertson gives definitions, practical questions, and suggestions for how to broaden inclusivity not only in the realms of gender and sexuality but also in socioeconomic and racial identities.

Smith, Avery. "Binary-Breaking Liturgy: Worship materials using inclusive language for people and expansive language for God." *Binary Breaking Liturgy* (blog). https://binarybreakingliturgy.com.

Some of my poems can be adapted for use in a worship space, but for more specifically tagged liturgy, Smith's site offers various writings recognizing and celebrating marginalized communities. All material is free to use; just be sure to credit them and their site.

Spong, John Shelby. *The Sins of Scripture: Exposing the Bible's Texts of Hate to Reveal the God of Love.* New York: HarperSanFrancisco, 2005.

Like Knust's book, Spong takes on quite a bit more than homosexuality, but he dedicates an entire section to the matter. Note that he focuses exclusively on the debate around "homosexuality" within Scripture rather than the full plethora of sexualities.

IDENTITY

American Psychological Association. "APA Resolution on Gender Identity Change Efforts." February 2021. https://www.apa.org/about/policy/resolution-gender-identity-change-efforts.pdf.

This announcement from the APA unequivocally derides any attempt at what is commonly called "conversion therapy" or any other medical or therapeutic means to alter someone's transgender status, calling such efforts not only wrong but actively harmful. The brief also recognizes that trans, nonbinary, and other diverse gender expressions are not mental disorders, a long-awaited reversal in a similar category to the decision declassifying homosexuality as a disorder in the 1970s.

Asexual Visibility and Education Network. "AVENwiki." http://wiki.asexuality.org/Main_Page.

With forums, articles, and definitions, this wiki houses all the basics for asexual information. While it is, being a wiki, edited by users, the Asexual Visibility and Education Network (AVEN) moderates content so that it is reliable and grounded. There are pages not only for those who are themselves ace but also for parents, family, and friends learning how to be supportive.

Chen, Angela. *Ace: What Asexuality Reveals about Desire, Society, and the Meaning of Sex.* Boston: Beacon Press, 2020.

Chen, herself asexual, explores the expectations of a default-allosexual mindset and how the narrative of sex as the primary expression of intimacy shapes our culture, language, and ideas about each other. Through memoir, journalistic investigation, and interviews with other asexual people, Chen draws forward important questions about how we do and do not create space for the deep human connections of the ace community.

Connell, R. W. *Masculinities.* 2nd ed. Berkeley: University of California Press, 2005.

Connell uses ethnography and psychology to show the arc of masculinity as a social construct. He also examines how sexuality and masculine identity complicate each other, asserting that masculinity is not a monolithic concept but a varied category in which patriarchy and politics have wide-ranging consequences. This second edition has a more global focus in recognition that gender is practiced differently in different cultures.

Duron, Lori. *Raising My Rainbow.* New York: Broadway Books, 2013.

This memoir/advice book is based in Duron's blog about her adventures raising a gender-nonconforming child, self-described as "a boy who likes girl stuff." The book uses humor and honesty to speak into the ways prescribed masculinities often stifle the emotional and creative capabilities of boys as they grow into men. While this is geared toward parents, those who are themselves gender-nonconforming may find value in the ways Duron navigates her allyship of her son and begins to overcome her own assumptions of what children should love and why.

Finke, Leigh, ed. *Queerfully and Wonderfully Made: A Guide for LGBTQ+ Christian Teens.* Minneapolis: Beaming Books, 2020.

While targeted toward teens raised in Christian environments or connected to the Christian church, this book deals primarily with the questions of "how, what, why" that are so crucial to coming out. Sex, bullying, pop culture representation, how to find supportive communities, and navigating faith are all part of this informally written introduction that serves up both honesty and compassion.

Gender Spectrum. "Gender Spectrum Resources." https://www.gender-spectrum.org/.

The primary focus of Gender Spectrum's database is children and teens and those who support them, but the support system is not just parents and family—there are resources for faith communities, mental health professionals, camp leaders, teachers, and those in the social services. Chat groups, conversation guides, and informational videos are the very beginning of all this has to offer, as well as places for children and teens to ask questions and find answers as they discover themselves.

Human Rights Campaign. "Resources." https://www.hrc.org/resources.

HRC focuses entirely on working toward equal rights for LGBTQ+ people around the world and has collected an impressive array of reading for free access. Topics include health, the intersection of sexuality and race, legal issues, parenting, religion, and tips on how to live into one's identity fully.

Moon, Allison and KD Diamond. *Girl Sex* 101. Lunatic Ink (lunaticink. com), 2014.

Through story, illustration, and a heaping dose of humor, Moon and her cadre of anecdotalists frankly discuss sexuality between women of all types, including trans women at all stages. Anatomy, expectations, consent conversations, sexual safety, and navigating the identity of same-sex attraction come with the air of an older sister imparting solid wisdom.

The Trevor Project. "Resources." https://www.thetrevorproject.org/ resources.

Founded specifically to answer the high rates of suicide among LGBTQ+ teens, The Trevor Project now serves as an educational and advocational hub of rainbow support. This page includes readings and connections around mental health (with 24/7 counseling available) as well as information for allies and parents. There's also a service called Trevor Space that links LGBTQ+ teens around the world in an affirming, online community.

POETRY

De la Cruz, San Juan. *The Poems of St. John of the Cross.* Translated by John Frederick Nims. Chicago: University of Chicago Press, 1979.

Most famously known for his work on the "dark night of the soul," the Spanish saint John of the Cross's poems evoke the mystery of faith seen through a glass dimly. This bilingual edition allows readers to compare the original medieval Spanish and see the richness of John's lyrical style.

Goldberg, Natalie. *Writing Down the Bones: Freeing the Writer Within.* Boston: Shambhala, 1986.

This was one of the textbooks for my very first formal poetry class, and while it was a couple decades old even then it has stood the test of time as a fabulous resource for how to get what's in your head onto paper. Goldberg's short essays dismantle the intimidating intensity of writing and present suggestions that tap into the creativity you already have.

Raffel, Burton. *How to Read a Poem.* New York: Meridian, 1984.

As it says on the tin, this overview delves into the specifics of breaking down poetry around rhythm, meter, metaphor, line breaks, and so on. The writing style is somewhat informal, meaning you'll get the author's opinion on a poem along with his professional understanding. There are a few examples of Eastern poetry, but for the most part this is limited to European examples.

slats. *Queering Lent.* CreateSpace Independent Publishing, 2017.

Written as a discipline of a poem a day during the season of Lent that precedes Easter, slats' heartbreaking earnestness about a fierce faith in God and a navigation of their trans self is the kind of poetry that pulls forth more poetry. If you're looking for more faith/identity lyricism, this is a very good place to find it.

Other poets to consider who write around the notion of religion, identity, or both:

John Donne, Emily Dickinson, Annie Dillard, Peter Abelard, Maya Angelou, Phyllis Wheatley, Chinua Achebe, Aleida Rodriguez, Rachel Wiley (*Nothing Is Okay*), Thomas James (*Letters to a Stranger*), Vanessa

Angelica Villarreal (*Beast Meridian*), Danez Smith (*[insert] boy*), and Fatimah Asghar (*If They Come for Us*).

Appendix B

GLOSSARY

FAITH

Chancel: the part of a Christian church where the altar or communion table sits. It is often raised by a few steps or separated from the main part of the sanctuary by a screen and is where clergy and choir are usually located during a service.

Confession: a sacrament in the Roman Catholic Church and a holy act practiced informally in many Protestant denominations. Confession is the act of telling one's sins (in lesser or greater detail) to God or to another person as an accountability measure for changed behavior in future. Many congregations do communal confessions that recognize that there are grievances caused by societal sin.

Creed: from the Latin *credo*, "I believe." A creed is a short statement of an individual's or group's beliefs, usually about theological tenets. See, for example, the Apostles' Creed or the Nicene Creed.

Liturgy: from the Greek term *leitourgia*, "work of the people." Liturgy commonly means the shared language spoken by the congregation and the worship leaders during a worship service, including such things as a call to worship, a confession, a congregational response, and the like.

Pulpit: the stand from which a sermon is traditionally delivered. In older churches, the pulpit was often elevated for sound carriage and clear sight-lines, but with the invention of electronic sound systems pulpits tend to sit on the chancel itself. Pulpits are usually more ornate than lecterns, which are smaller podiums, and are sometimes reserved for the preacher only with all other liturgy delivered from the lectern. Some churches only have one stand and use pulpit and lectern interchangeably to refer to it.

IDENTITY

AFAB: Assigned Female At Birth. Replaces the language of "born female."

Alloromantic: people who experience romantic attraction to one or more genders. Romantic attraction is not the same as sexual attraction and can come in all the same variations, so someone can be a biromantic hetero-sexual or an aromantic pansexual or any other combination.

Allosexual: people who experience sexual attraction to one or more genders; sometimes abbreviated "allo."

Ally: a person outside of the LGBTQ+ community who supports and advocates for the rights and protections of those within it. (Ally can also be used for those in this position with other minority communities in the areas of race, gender, and class.) It is wise never to name yourself as an ally but to wait for someone within the minority community to give that title to you. There can also be allies within the LGBTQ+ community for those of other identities, like a cisgender gay man who is an ally of trans people.

AMAB: Assigned Male At Birth. Replaces the language of "born male."

Aromantic: people who experience little to no romantic attraction; often abbreviated "aro."

Asexual: an umbrella term for people who experience little to no sexual attraction; often abbreviated "ace."

Bisexual: people who experience sexual attraction to at least two genders, including their own. Some people who experience attraction to more than two genders prefer "pansexual" while others continue using "bisexual;" it's a matter of choice for the person self-identifying. Please do not correct someone on their term for themselves. Often abbreviated "bi."

Butch: most often used within the lesbian community, this denotes a person who presents (looks and acts) as traditionally masculine.

Cisgender: identifying with the gender identity assigned at birth and not desirous of altering that identity.

Femme: most often used within the lesbian community, this denotes a person who presents (looks and acts) as traditionally feminine.

Gay: male-identifying person attracted to male-identifying people. This is sometimes also used as a catchall term for the entire LGBTQ+ community.

Gender: the social construction of a person's appearance long thought to be either male or female and now challenged as a scale or even a superfluous idea. Gender presentation can include physical appearance in body, clothing, or mannerisms, and vocal tone and cadence. The broader social implications of gendered things such as career tracks, toys, or hobbies are part of the discourse on gender and gendered identity.

Genderfluid: part of the nonbinary umbrella, genderfluid people often slide through the spectrum of gender presentation and can be socially recognized as male, female, neither, or both on any given day.

Heterosexual: experiencing sexual attraction to a single gender other than one's own.

Homosexual: experiencing sexual attraction to one's own gender.

Intersectionality: coined by Kimberle Crenshaw in the 1980s, this names the reality that different layers of oppression and discrimination do not exist separately from each other and alter the way such things are experienced. For example, a middle-class black trans woman who lives at the intersection of race, class, and gender identities has a different experience of discrimination than an upper-class white trans woman.

Intersex: an umbrella term for those who are born with sexual characteristics, internal or external, that do not fit completely in the male/female binary. Historically, births with the external markers of both sexes were "corrected" as soon as possible so that the child would fit the binary; now, people are learning not to see this as a defect to be altered but as a part of the person's physical identity.

Lesbian: woman-identifying person attracted to women-identifying people.

LGBT, LBGTQ, LGBTQIA+: although these are used interchangeably, each letter stands for a specific subgroup within the community of sexual and gender minorities. Lesbian, Gay, Bisexual, and Transgender are the most common terms but are not all-inclusive of the community; Q usually stands for Queer but can also mean Questioning. There is disagreement on whether Q is inclusive or whether it is its own identity in addition to other letters (many people within the community claim more than one letter in their self-descriptions). Intersex and Asexual/Agender/Aromantic people are divided as to whether they are truly welcome under the sexual and gender minority umbrella represented by the common use of the letters. There have been other shorthands developed for the community such as QUILTBAG (Queer/Questioning, Undecided, Intersex, Lesbian, Trans, Bisexual, Asexual/Agender/Aromantic, Gay) or Rainbow Community that have not gained as much popular traction. Increasingly, LGBTQ+ is the preferred acronym in scholastic and medical reference as well as broader online forums.

Nonbinary: an umbrella term for people who do not feel fully identified by "male" or "female" genders but feel more represented by both, neither, or some combination.

Pansexual: person experiencing sexual attraction to all genders.

Polysexual: person desiring simultaneous relationships with more than one other person.

Queer: a catchall term for identities historically deemed "other" and intended as a reclamation of the homophobic slur from the 20th century. Queer people can be queer due to sexuality, gender identity, romantic attraction, or any number of other markers that cause them to feel set apart from the societal "norm."

Transgender: an ever-expanding term for people whose gender identity differs from the one assigned at birth. Trans people can have gender affirming surgery or not, can present as an alternative gender or not, and can be on hormone therapy or not. This term has largely replaced the more outdated "transsexual."

POETRY

Alliteration: the repetition of a single consonantal sound within a phrase; for example, "the sea shore's slithering snakes slept."

Assonance: the matching of vowel sounds or diphthongs within neighboring words; for example, "the light of a fire in the blind eye."

Feet: the repeated segments of stressed and unstressed syllables in poetry that, with meter, create the rhythm of the piece. A longer line has more feet than a shorter one. Feet in English poetry most commonly have two (iambs and trochees) or three (dactyls and trochees) feet.

Form: the physical structure of a poem and its rhythm and rhyme schemes. The named forms have specific requirements in order to be classed within that name and there are many, many named forms. A few examples include tanka, found poetry, cinquains, sonnets, rondels, triolets, haiku, villanelles, limericks, elegies, sestinas, terzanelles, dodoitsu, sijo, bref doubles, acrostics, ballades, slam poetry, qasida, and narrative poetry. Poetry that does not adhere to a set form (has no specified feet or meter) is called "free verse" poetry.

Meter: the number of feet per line. In English poetry, numbers are named with Greek terminology, so lines can be dimeter, trimeter, tetrameter, pentameter, and so on. The most common meter in English poetry is pentameter, popularized and ingrained by William Shakespeare's work that is often in iambic pentameter.

Poem: a rhythmic and usually visually evocative style of writing that can include formal strictures such as rhyme, meter, and rhythm or can stylistically ignore these.

Prose: written or spoken language without deliberate rhythmic or metrical structure.

Rhyme: the matching of sounds often but not necessarily at the ends of lines in poetry; for example, "the art of the heart."